Donal Neary SJ

COMMUNION REFLECTIONS
FOR
SUNDAYS AND HOLY DAYS

YEAR C

GW00712296

VERITAS

First published 1997 by
Veritas Publications
7-8 Lower Abbey Street
Dublin 1

Copyright © Donal Neary SJ, 1997

ISBN 1 85390 337 X

British Library Cataloguing
in Publication Data.
A catalogue record for
this book is available
from the British Library.

Cover design by Banahan McManus
Printed in the Republic of Ireland by Criterion Press Ltd, Dublin

CONTENTS

INTRODUCTION

Communion Reflections For Sundays and Holy Days of Year C presents short reflections, mostly based on the scripture of the day, which are suitable for reading after Communion. Sometimes the reflection is centred on the feast of the day or on a general aspect of the Christian life.

Many people have noted that the Mass can 'end very suddenly', and there is need for a wide variety of reflections which may sum up and link the readings, the theme of the feast and the Mass. They value highly the inclusion of a Communion reflection, read in the quiet time and space of the Mass after Communion has finished, not while people are on the way to Communion.

On reading the Communion reflection

In introducing people to reading the Communion reflection, some attention might be paid to the differences between reading meditations, praying a prayer, preaching a homily and proclaiming the Scripture.

A Communion reflection is to be shared, rather than proclaimed or preached. This affects the tone of voice, the mood communicated through reading, the speed of reading and the method of preparation. A reflection will be read slowly. In cases where some line of the Scripture is repeated, two voices might be used. Repetitions of words will be noted, and they then sink into the heart. Gently and softly, prayerfully and slowly, are words the reader of the Communion reflection might recall when reading and preparing to read.

Careful preparation is more necessary for Communion reflections than for other liturgical readings which may be more familiar. The Communion reflection is new to both reader and listener, and thus needs careful and prayerful preparation. The reader of a Communion reflection should have the text well in advance of a liturgy and have time to pray over it.

Many people find the use of music in the background to Communion reflections intrusive. Others find it creates a mood of reflection. If music is used in the background, it needs to be such that does not distract from the reflection. Thus an instrument played too loudly or the music of a well-known hymn can distract from the content of the Communion reflection.

Communion Reflections For Sundays and Holy Days may also be used for private prayer; many of the reflections might be used also on other liturgical occasions, fitting similar themes or Scripture readings. May they enhance the liturgy with personal reflection on the great mysteries of our faith and thus bring the reader personally closer to the Lord Jesus whose death and resurrection is the theme of every Christian Liturgy.

FIRST SUNDAY OF ADVENT

Another Christmas

Advent is waiting for the birth of Jesus,
but it's a strange waiting;
we are waiting each year
for someone we know is here!

We recall in Advent
that the Lord Jesus has come among us,
is present all the time
and will come again in glory.

He is the child who is born each year,
for the world always needs its God and saviour.
He is the child awaited each year,
for our lives are new each year,
and we need him
in different ways at different stages of life,
and the world has different needs of God
at different times.

We need the child of peace to be born
in our wars and violence,
the child of wisdom
in our search for truth and meaning,
the child of gentleness
in a world which can be harsh and greedy.

We need to know in Jesus
that birth and life
are the most precious gifts of God,
and that in the birth of Jesus each year,
is the everlasting promise of God
to be with us.

And Advent looks ahead,
letting us see that the life of Jesus is never over,
that the truth of Jesus is always spoken,
and that he will one day be seen in glory.

For we are people of Advent and Easter,
of waiting and of resurrection;
we are people of earth and Heaven,
as he is the Son of God and Son of Mary,
and leads us through our life on earth
to the eternal glory of Heaven.

SECOND SUNDAY OF ADVENT

Prepare the Way

Everything we do
can prepare the way for God.
For God makes his home among us,
and Jesus is born to dwell within each of us.

In love and in friendship,
there is the meeting-place of God and people,
as in the love and the promise of Mary
there was the space for God to become one of us.

In our human love
we prepare the way for the love of God,
in our human forgiveness
we prepare the way for the forgiveness of God,
in our human compassion
we prepare the way for the compassion of God.

Our human work for the betterment of people
prepares the way for the justice of God,
and our human way of reconciliation
for the grace of reconciliation of God and his people.

In love, forgiveness and compassion
we are sharing in the very life of God.

Without our co-operation,
there can be no justice of God,
no reconciliation of God,
no speaking of the word of God,

for without our voice the word of God is silent.

Advent invites us to choose love,
to commit our lives
to prepare the way for God.

It is our faith,
a faith born of love,
a faith born in the everyday
as Jesus was born of Mary,
that the Lord is born each year
in the desire of his people
to live within the love of God
and share this love in life.

THIRD SUNDAY OF ADVENT

The Good News

In the gospel of Jesus
there is the good news
that we are children of God
and that we are called together
into the love of God.

We are called to a
faith that is personal
and connected to the faith of others,
so that we have a care for the poor,
and for all in their times of need.

We are to give what we have,
to those who have not enough.
Those who have two tunics
give to those who have none.

And in giving to those who are needy,
we are giving to the needy Christ.

He is cold in those who are unclothed,
hungry in those who are starving,
lonely in those who are alone,
victimised in those who are bullied and abused.

He rejoices with us in good times,
and sympathises with us in our sorrow.

The Lord Jesus
was born among us
poor, rejected by many,
and loved by Mary and Joseph.

He himself, before he can speak,
is good news.
He is Son of God and one of us –
we await his birth this year
so that we can be reborn ourselves,
and each of us
can be the good news of God,

reborn in our conviction that
all men and women are brothers and sisters,
that all are children of God
and that all will share the joy of God,
when Jesus comes again in glory.

FOURTH SUNDAY OF ADVENT

Mary – Mother and Friend

A very human side of Mary –
after she knew she was to be the mother of God,
Mary visited her cousin Elizabeth,
an older woman who herself was expecting her first child.

She needed to talk with someone –
her hopes, her fears, her anxieties
and the puzzlement
of her mysterious visit from God,
and what God asked her to become –
the mother of Jesus.

And she knew her cousin would be the same.
Elizabeth, too, needed to talk over
her hopes, her fears, her anxieties
and the puzzlement
of her mysterious visit from God.

Like we all do:
There are times in life we need to talk,
and we need someone to listen.

If we're out in the cold,
we need the warmth of
someone else's sympathy, understanding,
someone just to listen, to be there,
and maybe to give a bit of advice.
And when we're very happy,
feel like dancing around the room or the fields,
we like to share that too.

They helped each other grow in their faith,
in what God had given to them
and what God was asking of them,

and they helped each other trust
that what the Lord promised them
would be fulfilled.

There are times in life when we need
more than someone to listen to us;
we need others to share their story
and help us trust.
We also need faith:

She knew that God would not leave her alone
when times would be rough and painful.
She knew that God would be there,
through people like Elizabeth now,
like the shepherds at the birth,
like John at the foot of the Cross.
She knew that God had called her,
and she could welcome his call with courage.

CHRISTMAS VIGIL

All are welcome

It's a good word, *welcome,*
a word of warmth, acceptance,
forgiveness, joy,
from one to another,
welcoming you as you are.

All are welcome to the birthplace of Jesus,
the child not old enough to know
but young enough to be amazed.
All of us, young and old,
with questions about life's direction and meaning,
and hearts wanting acceptance.
Parents seeing a familiar role in Mary and Joseph,
an old person with memories and fears,
and all who are trying to put together
the joy and sadness of life:
of every age and race,
all are welcome.

Sinner and saint, weak and strong, wounded and healed,
bend low enough to join God's Christmas party.
God came to his people and welcomed them
to the stable of Bethlehem,

a birthplace too small to welcome the world's goods,
but big enough to welcome everyone's goodness,
too small to welcome the world's goods,
but big enough to accept the selfishness of all who came,
sending his Son through Mary and with Joseph,
telling shepherds who would bring their poverty
and others who would bring their wealth,
and none but God would know which gifts were most
worthy.

The shepherds got it right;
They got there first,
burdened by no expensive gifts,
because they were empty enough in soul
to know they had nothing to bring but themselves.

For the true welcome welcomes the person, not the gift;
the best gift you can give this night is yourself.
You are welcomed as you are,
God's child of delight,
each of us heartily wanted
and warmly welcomed.

May we be blessed this night,
a night of welcome:
may we know we are loved as we are,
God delighting in each of us,
as he delighted in Jesus,
Son of Mary, Son of God.

CHRISTMAS DAY

A gift for the child of Christmas

And the shepherds came,
and it doesn't say they brought anything –
no lamb, no hay, no food,
no gifts for the child.

Yet they were the honoured guests,
for we need to bring nothing to God
except the gift all can bring.

We bring ourselves,
our love.

And even though love has its flaws,
and is not perfect,
yet it is the choicest gift of all.

In it God recognises us at our best,
and he recognises the likeness of his Son.

He welcomes our love with its flaws,
as when we think we're loving someone
when we are more filling our own needs;
loving someone only to fill loneliness
or for what another can give.

No love is perfect;
every effort to love is a gift for God.
The relationships that last
with all their ups and down
are our Christmas gift to the child of God.
And every hug from a baby child
is a beginning of our deepest desire –
to love and be loved.
In the broken marriage and disappointed relationship

there was the effort to love;
every bond of parent and child –
even in the worst of relations –
is a bond of love.
But somewhere love got lost.

In the middle of all this
is the desire and effort,
even the struggle to love.

This desire and gift,
given by God,
is what we bring to Jesus this night.

And God delights in love.

THE HOLY FAMILY

Roots and wings

There's the old saying about the family –
families give us roots and wings,
a place of departure
and a place of return.

And it was like that for Jesus,
Mary and Joseph.

In the temple
Jesus realised that his family was bigger
than his home and extended family;
that his responsibility was not just
to his family, but to God.

And isn't it like that for all of us?
Children move from being totally dependent
to finding their own way through life,
with new relationships,
growing old enough
eventually to make their own decisions
and moving out to form their own families;
searching from within the faith handed on to them
to find a faith that is their own.

We need to look to our roots in different ways
at different ages and challenges of life.

Our wings, woven in the family,
take us to new spaces of life;
and our roots will always nourish us –
the roots of home and the people of home,
as fresh to us as the newly-ironed shirt,
as warm as the home-baked food,
as deep as the soil of the land of home.

Jesus found those roots again,
as he returned home
to Mary and Joseph,
and there grew in wisdom and stature
and in favour with God and people.

SECOND SUNDAY AFTER CHRISTMAS

The Way, the Truth and the Life

Who is this child?
The Light who guides our way,
The Word who is our truth,
the One in whom all have life.

Jesus is the way that guides our steps,
a hand that holds us on life's journey,
a direction for our desires and hopes,

an invitation to be involved with others,
for he himself has walked the way of friendship;
encouragement in times of trouble,
for he has walked the way of pain;
a signpost through life and into eternity,
for he walked the way of resurrection.

Jesus is the truth that enlightens our minds,
speaking the word of God
in times of confusion and trouble,

opening the mind to truth
when many options are presented,

giving the gift of meaning to life
when loss and anxiety may take over,
for he himself lived in the light of God.

And the Lord Jesus is our life,
in his words and gestures of love,
in his call to love and service,

sharing the bread of life
in the Eucharist of nourishment

sharing the life of forgiveness
in times of guilt and sin and failings.

Who is this child?
The Word who is our truth,
the Light who guides our way,
the Life who promises love forever.

THE BAPTISM OF OUR LORD

Sons and daughters of God

Into the water of the Jordan
Jesus descended,
as he had descended from heaven to earth,
as he would later descend to the underworld;

he entered fully into the depths of the river,
into the depths of humanity,
into everything that is human
and then he heard the words of God,
You are my Son, the Beloved.

A big moment for Jesus,
a moment when he knew God was with him,
that he was loved and was on the path of God.

Moments like when we knew we were loved by God,
on a mountain walk,
a stroll by the sea,
a time of prayer,
a conversation with a friend,
a time when we knew we were helping someone,
times when we have plunged into the depths
and discovered the love of God.

Moments like illness and bereavement,
anxiety about a child or a parent,
staying with someone in times of trouble:
then we have discovered something
not always seen or heard,
a faith born from the depths
of our human experience
that we are sons and daughters of God.

In entering human life fully
we find the presence of the Divine,
for all that is human is created by God,
and in human love, compassion,
endurance and care,
we find God's dwelling-place,
and we know our home is with him.

FIRST SUNDAY IN LENT

Following the way of Jesus

As we set our feet on the path of Jesus,
temptations will come to follow other paths,
to give our energy and commitment to other ways,
to look for life and happiness away from God.

The temptation to Jesus was
to live for himself;
like the instinct in each of us
to see ourselves as number one.
Jesus' conviction, spread in his works
of healing the sick in mind and body,
of consoling people in all sorts of situations,
and teaching the way to God,
and finally in his death on the Cross,
is that true fulfilment
is in being men and women of God for others.

He was son of God for us,
not for himself;
the temptation was
to turn the spotlight on himself,
and accept a life of comfort,
concerned with honour, wealth and power.

The gifts of personality that each of has
are to fit us for our journey of life,
and to be shared with all we meet on
the journey of life we share.

Our wealth, learning, talents –
all we have received in our upbringing,
all we have received from God –
are to enrich not only ourselves,
but are given for the life of the world.

Called by God to be
men and women for others,
we may be tempted to use
our love and our talents,
even faith and religion,
just for ourselves.

May we walk in the path of true life,
may we create a world of equality and justice,
where the dignity of people
is valued as much as the dignity of God.

In Jesus we are brothers and sisters,
men and women for others.
Together may we walk on the
path of life eternal.

SECOND SUNDAY OF LENT

This is my Son, listen to him.

In the cloud and mist the disciples were afraid.
They had climbed the mountain with Jesus,
as they had been through tough times with him –
times when people rejected him,
mocked his sermons in the synagogue,
condemned his compassion for people,
and now they had seen his glory –
they had seen him at the best humanity could offer
and they had seen what divinity looked like,
the glory of God on the face of Jesus.

We journey like that –
mountain steepness and boulders tire us,
the summit seems far off,
like trying to understand those we love,
or trying to create some sort of a better world,
or trying to live up to the call of God.

And we glimpse glory
like when the mists lifts on a mountain,
the glory of love and of reconciliation,
or the glory of God's nearness in prayer.

If we're lost in a mountain mist
we get afraid –
and we get afraid in the mists of life –
of losing our way, our health, our securities.
There are times when we glimpse
in the lifting of the mist
that God is with us
on all of the journey,

caring for us in all troubles,
offering us the word of life,

naming each of us
his beloved child.

May we listen to his word,
the word of comfort in trouble,
of challenge in our ease,
of faithfulness always.

THIRD SUNDAY OF LENT

Another chance

Jesus told a story about
someone coming to a fig tree
and looking for fruit,
and wanting it cut down because it was barren.
But he was persuaded to give it another chance.

Jesus liked that story
because he's the person of another chance.

With his friends
there was always the chance
to turn around,
become whole again
and follow him anew,
even after denial and cowardice.

He looks ahead of us
on our path of life
and sees a new way,
another chance out of failure,
a new conversion from sin.

Our book of life is never closed for Jesus,
our disk of life is never full,
the song of our life is never sung out.

We are not programmed like on a computer,
nor is our life's plan pressed on a compact disc.
We are people who can always change,
become strong again, walk confident,
hand-in-hand with God.

As Jesus sees us as people who may change and grow,
may we see others in the same light.

FOURTH SUNDAY OF LENT

He welcomes sinners and eats with them.

Two types of people welcomed by Jesus:
one, the younger son
who had gone away,
squandered his life
and returned empty.

Those times of life
we know were wasted and were wrong,
use of people or wealth or life just for ourselves,
failure to look after those in our care,
or neglect of God and the things of God.

Jesus offers always
the bread of acceptance and forgiveness,
the invitation to make always a new start,
the insight that the future can always be more whole.
A welcome to the wasted and battered sides of life,
in his mercy and forgiveness.

And a welcome for the elder son:
the one who had done everything right,
but could not say 'I have sinned',
who had always tried to be faithful,
who had practised his religion,
but seemed to do so in isolation,
for he could not welcome with compassion
the brother who returned home.

A welcome, too, for the sin of uninvolvement,
of caring first for self and not for others,
and an invitation to join all at the celebration
of reconciliation and forgiveness.

For God is the one who can give all,
to the one who returns to his embrace
and to the one who was always in his embrace.
for he welcomes sinners and eats with them.

FIFTH SUNDAY OF LENT

And Jesus started writing on the ground with his finger.

People have wondered and imagined
what Jesus wrote when they asked him
to condemn the woman.

Whatever he wrote
encouraged the woman to stay with him,
and put some pressure on the accusers to move away.

Maybe he just doodled – wrote nothing sensible?

Or did he write so – that the woman could see –
'Stay here, I am with you'.
And the woman knew,
like all of us know when we're in trouble,
that Jesus is on our side.

Or did he write so that the onlookers could see –
'Change your hearts,
be renewed,
forgive in your hearts
and come back – sin no more'.

Maybe he wrote what he later said –
'I do not condemn you, sin no more.'
And all knew they were in the presence
of love, forgiveness and acceptance.

Some, like the woman, could take this
and stayed to get to know this Jesus.
Others, like the accusers, went away,
but maybe they came back later,
to get to know this Jesus.

No matter what,
we know that he will stay with each of us,
Eucharist each day,
forgiveness and acceptance
all the days of our life.

PASSION SUNDAY

*A number of reflections are given for Passion Sunday
which may be used on other days of Holy Week.*

1. And he carried our burdens.

This is your friend, my friend, on the Cross.
We were on the road to Calvary with him,
and went out to help him carry his cross.
We spoke with him.
We remembered our sins and how we let him down,
and he just gently murmured,
'Remember the story I told you about the prodigal son'.
Always thinking of us, always a friend, always loving.
'Tell all', he said, 'Your sins are forgiven.'

And he carried our burdens.

We saw his bleeding face and hands
and thought of women who are battered,
and boys and girls who are abused,
and men who are tortured,
and it all seemed the same body.
And our own sufferings seemed to be in his body too.
Carrying the cross of us all.

And he carried our burdens.

Jesus had no crucified Lord to support him at his death.
Maybe Mary spoke a prayer for him, and he heard it,
for they say hearing is the last of our senses to go.
He didn't have the help at death which we have –
the example of our suffering Lord.

He glimpsed somewhere in the distance
the faces of friends and the caring look of his mother.
May we know in death and suffering

the cross of Jesus,
the risen glory of Jesus,
our cross, our risen glory.

And he carried our burdens.

2. It was night

It was night.
After Judas left
he took the piece of bread
and left his wine unfinished,
for his hour of betrayal had come –
the night of betrayal,
the night of confusion,
the night of hatred.
The night of God.
Not alone was the night dark,
but so was the heart of Jesus.
'Deeply disturbed'
is how his friend John remembers him that night.

Judas, one he spent time with,
shared himself with,
would hand him over.
Peter, one he called friend,
one he guided in the way of God,
would deny him.

It was the darkness of rejection.
Like the darkness felt when marriage is breaking up,
when children are letting you down,
or parents have acted with violence,
when there's bereavement and terminal pain,
when another you love is taken away.
Then you say 'It is night'.
As surely as each day has its darkness
every life too has its darkness.

And as sure as there is light within night's darkness,
there is light in life's darkness.

Fear of the future,
let-down at the past,
isolation in the present;
all we share of the night.

In the midst of our darkness can we remember
that in this night Jesus was glorified?

We sing silent night at Christmas, holy night;
we sing night of sadness now, and it is still holy night;
for within this darkness is the glimmer of God's light.

3. Mary anointed him

There's generosity in Mary's ointment;
the fragrant oil bathed her saviour's tiredness.
The house was filled with the scent of the ointment,
like the fragrance of burning oil or flowers filling a room.
It was the fragrance
of thoughtfulness, of love, of generosity.

Maybe on the road to Calvary Jesus would remember this
     fragrance,
and in the smell of blood, sweat and crowds,
a waft of perfumed scent would touch his nostrils
– a memory of friendship and care which was still there
even though those who anointed him were absent –
and he'd know there are those who care, who understand
and who are open to receive his love.
Peace of spirit in the pain of body.

The Passion begins with generosity
and it's the hour of the generous love of God:
conviction, compassion, justice, love
poured out for everyone,

for those present and for those to come,
for those who believe and for those who mock,
for those who accept and for those who reject,
for John and Mary, the high priest and the thief.
It is the hour of the greatest love ever known;
and every self-sacrificing love smells sweet on Calvary:
the love of Jesus and the love of a friend,
the love of Mary, John and his relatives
like the love of mother, father and family,
the love of a thief and the unexpected love of someone.

We have met him, known him, loved him,
in the circle of love we inhabit ourselves,
we do not have him with us as then in human form,
but we do have him with us now as love.

EASTER SUNDAY

New life

And the tomb was empty.
It's empty not because we took him out,
but because God called him
into new, triumphant, risen life.
Jesus is alive.

We don't expect much change in a tomb,
only that the body will rot and disintegrate.
A place that is cold, empty, fearful.
We don't think of it as a place of life,
yet in the tomb Jesus was called

from the coldness of death to the warmth of new life,
from the emptiness of death to the fullness of new
    consolation,
from the dread of nothingness to the confidence of new
    mission.

The clothes left behind,
rolled up,
never to be used again.
For life is new,
and on a new day
we wear new clothes.

The clothes of death give way to the bright colours of
    resurrection,
and injustice gives way to care and compassion,
hurt and violence to reconciliation.
The hand of friendship is stretched out to another,
and people just try to make it together.

Old clothes no longer needed,
angers long smouldering put out

with new hope, new life
and a new vision of God.
And fears once crippling new life
evaporate into confidence
the wearers are raised to new life,
new love and work for God.

For the tomb of Jesus is the place of light
and the tomb of Jesus is the space of eternity.

SECOND SUNDAY OF EASTER

Many other signs

They remembered some things Jesus did,
wrote down others,
but there were more.

There are other books where the signs of Jesus are
    written,
the books of everyone's life.
You and I are the signs of Jesus:

the ordinary kindnesses of an ordinary day,
like a message brought for a housebound person,
like the daily care of father and mother,
the care of children for parents and family,
signs of the love and the care of Jesus.

The signs that Jesus is alive:
remembering the bereaved and the sick,
creating employment and good housing,
helping the work of others in a developing country;
signs of the love and care of Jesus,
that he is raised from death,
and we are writing the resurrection story for today.

And in the suffering of people
we write the words of the risen Lord,
especially the support given where
people suffer through others:
the mother whose child is in prison,
the family suffering through addictions and violence,
the memory of the violence or greed of others;
when support is offered and given,
there is the gospel written again for today.

There were many other signs that Jesus worked
and the disciples saw,
but they are not recorded in the gospel.
They are recorded in the book of life,
yours and mine,
known only to those close to us
and to God himself.

THIRD SUNDAY OF EASTER

It is the Lord.

> They watched from the boat
> and looked to the shore:
> an early dawn,
> maybe a mist till the sun got strong,
> and a figure in the mist.
>
> It was Jesus but they did not recognise him.
> then they picked up some words from the shore
> and it began to dawn –
> they knew him by his words of friendship and life,
> and later would know him in the bread of life.
>
> It is the Lord:
> This can be said:
> when we are surprised by the peace of prayer,
> by the love of a friend,
> by the care shown us when we need care,
> by the truth that enlightens our minds
> and the life that gives a lift to our hearts,
> and the care we offer to others.
>
> Not always clear:
> We search for the light of God
> in the twilight of doubt
> or the darkness of pain;
> we search for the peace of God
> in the violence of bitterness
> and in the guilt of our heart;
> we search for the generosity of God
> in our desire to do the best we can
> and in the needs of the world.
>
> Not always clear:
> If we search alone we do not find him.

We search and ponder about God
within our community of believers,
within our community of love,
and within the community of those
who wish to create with Jesus
a world of justice and peace,
of forgiveness and reconciliation,
of love and joy.

It is the Lord
who takes the bread of life
and speaks the word of life
to give direction and nourishment for our journey –
Jesus, the God of earth,
the God of heaven.

FOURTH SUNDAY OF EASTER

No one can ever steal them from me.

We belong to him,
as closely as the stone belongs to a rock,
the water to a river,
the scent to perfume,
for without him we would be nothing.

We belong to him
as the shadow belongs to the sun,
as the taste belongs to the bread,
as the reflection belongs to the light,
for without him we would be nothing.

We belong to him
as a child to a parent –
loved, united
but each our own person.

We belong to him
as brothers and sisters belong to each other,
finding our family roots
in the family of God,
and each unique in our own personality.

We belong to him,
as earth belongs to heaven,
as the son Jesus belongs to his Father,
for as he and the Father are one,
so we are one with him,
and belong to God
because he belongs to God.

And because he has been born and lived among us,
the Word of God made flesh,
he belongs to us,

and we share his life,
as he humbled himself to share our life.

We belong to him when we sit with him in payer,
or when we share his work,
each in our own way,
according to our talents and our call in life,
of bringing on earth the kingdom of God.

FIFTH SUNDAY OF EASTER

Love one another as I have loved you.

It was one of those days.
Things had gone wrong all day –
some tensions at work,
annoyance with people,
criticism behind their backs –
one of those days.

The words sometimes go through my mind then:
Love one another as I have loved you.
They don't make it any easier,
but somehow it makes
things look a bit different,
and I think a bit more kindly
of another.

Sometimes it's the **love one another**
that I remember and that gets me.
Why should I love him?
Why should I care for her?
They don't seem to want to care for me.
And I hear,
in the ear of the mind and the memory of the heart,
the words of Jesus,
as I have loved you.

Your total love of me, Lord,
is like a tidal wave coming over me,
refreshing, cooling, drenching me
and that gives me another chance
to cool off hot words,
refresh tired judgements
and believe that,
as you love me,
you also love everyone.

Thanks for the words:
Love one another as I have loved you.
They spur me on,
cool me down,
centre me and focus me
on the gift of love and hope
that is your gift to me.

FEAST OF THE ASCENSION OF OUR LORD

The link of heaven and earth

As Jesus departs from us,
there is a new link between heaven and earth,
and we are present in heaven.

He brings our sufferings,
marked in the wounds of hands, feet and side.
He brings our sin,
which has wounded him
and through his wounds we are healed.
He gives on earth
the healing of heaven.

He brings our hopes,
alive in his risen body;
our hopes that good will overcome evil,
that justice will prevail over greed,
and that love is the most powerful force we know.
He brings with him
our hope that we will live forever,
and because he lives now in eternity,
we know we too shall live,
alive to joy and peace,
in the circle of love which is the home of God.

God's glory is Jesus fully alive,
God's glory is men and women fully alive,
fully alive to love,
to the call of God,
and to the life we can share with each other.
Each of us is the glory of God,
glimpsed partly here,
to be fully enjoyed in heaven.

Where Jesus is,
we shall follow.

SEVENTH SUNDAY OF EASTER

Peace I leave you, my own peace I give you.

Don't we all want this gift of peace?
Peace in our hearts,
the Easter gift of the risen Lord,
the promise of the Spirit of God.

The promises of Jesus
do not seem to include
wealth, employment,
freedom from tension, success,
health for ever, or freedom from worry,
nor many more things we hope and pray for.

Peace I leave you, my own peace I give you.

So what is this peace?
The peace that nobody can take away:

the peace of being valued for who I am,
of being at home with other people,
of letting go past hurts,
of doing what I know to be right,
of being convinced of eternity,

of being loved,
and of knowing the possibility of love –
love given, promised and shared,
of knowing that love and life will last forever,
and the peace of forgiveness when I fail.

The peace of being always with
someone who totally loves us,
and believes in us:
who sees us and loves us as we are,
and calls us to be what we can be.

And the peace of knowing
that with Jesus,
we can create in love
a world according to the mind of God.

Peace I leave you, my own peace I give you.

PENTECOST SUNDAY

Renew – refresh

Holy Spirit,
refresh the face of the earth;
refresh like the cool wind through humid air,
refresh like cooling rain in stagnant water,
refresh like greenery in the burnt desert –
and refresh tired hopes,
dull love,
broken trust,
with gentle confidence
with new visions of each other,
with a belief in goodness.
refresh and renew us.

Refresh our countries,
with compassion in politics,
with peace based on justice,
with respect for the dignity of all,
and a genuine care for those in need,
and policies to end inequality.

Refresh families with tolerance,
communities with openness,
whole neighbourhoods with involvement;

Refresh our prayer with your love,
our sorrow with your forgiveness,
our generosity with your call.

Refresh us,
renew us,
renew the face of the earth.

SECOND SUNDAY IN ORDINARY TIME

Things can change.

Things can change:
water can become wine,
families can be reconciled,
justice can replace violence
peace can cover the land.

And people can change
when they get a chance.
Love can change
hardness of heart into compassion,
prayer can change
a selfish style of life into generosity.

With the touch of Jesus
water can change to wine,
and men and women can change,
and become more like God.

God sees us as we are,
and as we can be.

As the water was changed
at the word of Jesus
and the prayer of Mary,
so too the world can change
at the word of Jesus,
made active through us,
and the prayer of Mary
and of his followers.

We are not stuck in the present,
nor are we prisoners of the past.
The followers of Jesus
are people with a future.

We are the people of the resurrection.

And so this day we make a prayer
for justice where there is inequality,
for peace where there is violence,
for love where there is hate.
And all this can happen,
when we try to put on
the mind and heart of God.

THIRD SUNDAY IN ORDINARY TIME

With the power of the spirit

The spirit of a person is within the unique cluster
of gifts, exuberances, talents, loves, hopes,
worries, hurts, anxieties,
that makes each person
unique, never to be replaced.
It is what we remember of someone
who has left us.

Jesus spoke from the depths of his spirit,
from what made him unique:
Son of God, Son of Mary,
Word of Heaven, Human Word,
Bread of God, Human Flesh,
for the life of the world,
and at the very last
he gave up his Spirit
that his Spirit might live:

the Spirit of wisdom to teach the true way of life,
the Spirit of compassion to reach out to all of us,
the Spirit of courage to follow through his work to the end,
the Spirit of gentleness to invite each to the embrace of God,
the Spirit of forgiveness to move on always to deeper love.
And this Spirit gave him power,
a power of conviction and of love
so that the ears of all were on his word.

This is the power of his people,
the Spirit he shares through all time.
What made him unique
still invites all of us
to be his people,
the community of believers,
the Church of God.

FOURTH SUNDAY IN ORDINARY TIME

They hustled him out of the town.

Jesus is for everyone.
Some thought they were the
favourites or chosen or privileged ones of God.
They couldn't accept that he was for the whole world,
not just for them.

God is for everyone
at every time of life –
for the child in helplessness and security,
for the adolescent in confusion and exuberance,
for the young adult in searching for and finding lasting
        love,
for the mid-adult in disappointment and in joy of
        children,
for the elderly in illness and in serenity –
let us give thanks to God,
for he is our God at all times and in all places.

And God is in all the places within ourselves,
our zones of body, mind and soul;
in that lonely place he is friend,
in that guilty place he is forgiveness,
in that shameful place he is affirmation,
in that joyful place he is happiness,
in that compassionate place he is mercy,
in that sharing place he is encouragement.

God is big enough to be for everyone;
he is weak enough to be for everyone.
And for this they wanted to get rid of Jesus,
God's presence among us
his faithfulness for always.

FIFTH SUNDAY IN ORDINARY TIME

From now on you will catch people.

Caught by a smile in a crowded room,
and you find the gathering is never the same;
caught by a loving touch
and you know you are not alone;
caught by a joke on you
and you know you are teased or mocked.

We are caught by the word of God
and our lives are changed,
like the friendship
or a chance meeting
that catches us unawares
can change our lives.

We are caught
by the compassion of God
so that we know we are always loved,
even when we cannot love ourselves.
We are caught by God's forgiveness
and know that nothing of the past
need catch us in nets of guilt;
caught by the call of God
and we know that God wants
to catch others through us.

We are invited, each of us,
into his service,
to be caught by
the beauty, joy,
challenge and freedom
of his invitation.

We know that we can be his followers,
into his service.

He catches us to be
his word and presence,
compassion and love
in the world of today.

SIXTH SUNDAY IN ORDINARY TIME

Blessed are we.

Blessed are people who have lost a lot –
isn't this what Jesus is saying?

People who have lost money and are poor,
who have lost love and who weep,
who have lost food and are hungry.

And we can think of people who have lost a lot,
who are refugees or out of work,
who are lonely or without friends,
and wonder what sort of happiness is this?

We can only ask if there have been times
when life seemed very empty
and yet there was peace.

When children leave home,
either because they want to or have to;
when husband or wife dies,
when marriage breaks up,
when family relationships go sour,
the soul and heart are opened,
and the love and care of God may enter.
Or in the middle of the pain and the disappointments,
we know that some other energy is around,
that gives another peace,
not in place of what we missed,
but alongside it.

And we begin to know
that there are many happinesses,
some can last, like love and convictions,
some last just a while, like youth and health,
some last forever, like faith, hope and love,

and one blessing nobody can take from us
is the relationship we have with God in Jesus,
for in all of life's experiences
is a space for the blessing of God.

SEVENTH SUNDAY IN ORDINARY TIME

Looking beyond the obvious

A tough message –
to love people we find difficult,
people who drive us mad,
or worse still, people who have wronged us.

And often the only motive
is the motive Jesus gives –
love others with the love of God.

God looks into the depths of
everyone's personality
and sees there what he has made.

Like an artist looks on a picture
or a photographer on a photo,
and you see there both what you did,
and what you tried to do.

Like a parent looks on a child
and sees in the child
the gift of their life,
and the love that goes beyond anything
done, said,
or not done, not said
by the child.

God looks on each of us
and sees in us his creation,
and what he sees and loves in Jesus,
he sees and loves in us.

And his eyes shine with compassion;
seeing beyond everything to the spark of life and light
that shines in us all.

Can we see with the eyes of God,
noticing and loving in everyone
the child of God?

EIGHTH SUNDAY IN ORDINARY TIME

Inside each of us

Inside each of us is a home,
where God and love may dwell.
A place of warmth and safety,
a place of welcome and forgiveness,
and there God makes his home.

Or inside each of us is a garden,
where God and love may grow.
Soil of beauty and colour
Of variety and growth,
and there God makes his home.

Our home needs care
and our garden needs tending,
and then they are places of love
and spaces of growth,

and others may live and grow
in our care and our love.

The next generation grows in the shade of the previous,
and we need to care for our home,
if others are to find safety there,
and if it is to be the dwelling-place of God.

And we need to nourish the garden
if the fruit is to be sound,
and the tree strong,
and others live in its shadow
and gather good fruit.

We are a mixture of good and bad,
and in prayer and love
we nourish the good

so that the home is loving
and the garden is sound.

And then we hope
that by our fruits
many will know
the reality of love in their lives.

NINTH SUNDAY IN ORDINARY TIME

Thanks for trust

So much of life is built on trust;
from the first moments of parents and child,
to the last breath when we give over our life
to what we do not know.

Love promised by husband and wife,
giving birth and bringing up a child,
are like putting our hands into the hands of God.

We can remember times in life when we were glad of
    faith:
a serious illness
and we believed in the closeness of God,
the death of those we loved
and we believed that they were with God,
children leaving home,
and we believed that God would look after them.

The hands that guide us are the hands of God,
hands that knew our life and love,
that knew pain and suffering,
that knew their need for the hands of
mother, father, friend.

The hands of God
are the wounded hands of Jesus.
In his pain and suffering,
in his rejection and loneliness,
in his hurt and need
he looked to trust in God his Father.

He knows our need of faith,
and he gives this gift of faith.

For faith we give thanks,
for the nearness of God and God's care,
for the nourishment of the Eucharist on life's journey,
for peace and help in prayer
and for the hands that lifted, touched and cared when
    needed.

For faith in life,
as everlasting as the sand on the seashore,
like the colour so essential to the flower,
we give thanks.

TENTH SUNDAY IN ORDINARY TIME

God has visited his people.

God is a visitor with gifts
arriving into our lives,
keeping nothing for himself,
wanting to give all away,
touching us with graces,
so that we are God's
gift-givers and grace-givers
to others.

His hands are full
with the gifts of life;
his heart is full
with the gift of compassion.

When the heart is broken
like the mother grieving for her son,
his whole being goes out in compassion;
he wants to give life,
and the life he gives
is for now and for eternity.

From his risen freedom,
victor over death and violence,
he promises that we will
walk eternally
in the life and love of God.

And his compassion –
caring, sympathetic and faithful –
reaches out to touch us
with the promise of encouragement,
with the promise of his presence,
with the promise of life eternal.

He has opened his door
in the life of Jesus
to grace his world with gifts.
We open our door to receive him,
and welcome his gifts
of new life and compassion
into our lives.

ELEVENTH SUNDAY IN ORDINARY TIME

All are invited to the Lord's table.

Inviting Jesus into life
is always a risk
For it means welcoming joyfully
the challenge of the gospel,
to live in justice, faith and compassion,
and to see Jesus in others.

Those we love and those we find difficult,
those we worry about and feel responsible for,
these are Jesus,
and those whose lives are wrecked or damaged
by society's neglect and greed,
these too are Jesus.

The child at home giving trouble,
The poor looking for some help – each is Jesus.
The student worried about an exam,
Husband or wife on a bad day – each is Jesus.

The child at home bringing joy and life,
A man or woman giving time to the poor – each is Jesus.
Young people offering talents and service to others,
The love of husband and wife – each is Jesus.

People who drive us mad,
people who have offended us a lot,
these are Jesus.
People who have let us down
and who have betrayed us –
these are Jesus.

And if we are at Jesus' table,
they will be there too.
The love of Jesus is all-inclusive:

you and I on our best days,
and also on our worst,
are included in this friendship, forgiveness and love.

All are invited to the table of Jesus,
all are welcome at the Eucharist,
all are forgiven,
all are called into a new life.

TWELFTH SUNDAY IN ORDINARY TIME

Who do you say that I am?

We call Jesus by many names
and we all have our own answer
to Jesus' question
Who do you say that I am?

We call him the child Jesus,
for he came among us like any of us,
born of his mother, helpless and weak,
needing the care we all want
at the beginning of life.

We call him Saviour
for his forgiveness offers us
a way not to let sin control us,
and his call to be disciples offers
a way to the world to overcome evil.

We call him Brother,
for he is like us
in everything but sin,
sharing our joys and sorrows,
wanting, like us, to love those we care for,
and longing for a world of equality and justice
for all his poor.

We call him Lord,
for he is the word of God
and Son of God,
who comes from heaven
to guide us home.
He is the truth of God
teaching the meaning of life
so that we will never be lost
in our search and hope for God.

We call him Friend,
for that is what he calls us.
He is the friend who shares himself with us,
who is the hand
of guidance and consolation
all the days of our life.

Who do you say that I am?
Friend, Lord, Brother, Child,
Son of God, Word of Life,
Way, Truth and Life.

THIRTEENTH SUNDAY IN ORDINARY TIME

Another step

Love always beckons another step.
Don't we know that from family life,
marriage, communities,
friendship?

Love may seem to have nowhere to lay its head
as we move from a secure place in love
to new trust, new challenges, new demands,
as children grow older,
a spouse gets ill,

And God may seem distant.

Love has to move on,
leaving dead ways of being with someone,
rising to new depths of conversation or care,
as families move out to marry and raise new families,
as our loved ones die or move away,

And God may seem remote.

Love looks back only in thanks.
For remembering past times with regret
is a way of living in the past,
like parents trying to pretend families are not grown up,
or people in mid-life hankering after youth.

Love enjoys the security and life of the present;
it is willing to move and grow with each other,
and it looks back only to say thanks
and bring the spirit of love –
grown and deepened from the past –
into the future.

And God is in love,
for he is the source and the energiser
of all true love.

FOURTEENTH SUNDAY IN ORDINARY TIME

The Good Samaritan

A lot can be learned about a people
from the stories they tell.

People who tell stories about their children
are letting us know how much they mean to them,
and this can be a way of remembering them
with love or with worry or prayers.

We know Jesus by the kind of stories he told,
and the Good Samaritan was one of his best.

Jesus could tell that story,
because like the man who watched others pass by
he had felt rejection and neglect himself;
and like the man who had been beaten up by thieves,
he had been mistreated by people who wanted to kill
      him.

So he knows what it's like
to be a victim of street violence,
or to queue for help and be passed by,
or to need any sort of sympathy and be ignored.
He knew what it was like to be bullied,
to be robbed, to be left alone.

And he knew what it was like to be helped
as the man in the ditch was helped,
and he remembered the care of Mary, his mother,
and those who looked after him on his journeys.
And he knew he would need help like that
when he was brought to his death.

And he was the type of person also who helped,
whose heart was moved with compassion

for the whole human race,
for you and me,
as was the heart of the Samaritan.

Jesus, who saves and calls us into his service,
tells about being the helper and the helped,
from the experiences of his own life.

That's something of what Jesus was like,
your friend and mine,
God of heaven and God of earth.

FIFTEENTH SUNDAY IN ORDINARY TIME

A person of peace

To bring peace among people
is one of life's greatest gifts.

People who are peacemakers
are the sons and daughters of God,
for they share in one of the biggest desires of God:
peace in the world,
peace in the community, the neighbourhood,
peace in the parish, and in the country,
peace in the heart of everyone.

To bring peace
we need to be at peace ourselves;

and the person of peace
is a person who knows his or her place,
and knows God's place in the world.

To be a person of peace
is to know that others have rights,
and that others have problems
that make them act the way they do,
and the person of peace
brings understanding and compassion
to the problems of others.

To be a person of peace
is to know that much in life
is outside our control.
We cannot turn back the sea
nor change the time of sunset,
and neither can we control the lives of others.

To be a person of peace
is to be engaged each day
in love and care
with the God of peace.

May we be instruments of God's peace,
for through each of us comes God's gift of peace for all.

SIXTEENTH SUNDAY IN ORDINARY TIME

The better part?

Time spent with people we love
is time treasured in our memory.

In the time together love grows,
friendships deepen
and people come to mean more to each other.

Time spent with each other in marriage
is the place where we feel
we are worthwhile, valued, loved.
Time spent with children is the place
from which love's energies
extend and reach out to children.

There are times when we must work
for and with each other,
when we must be busy,
and there are times for just being together.

Time spent with God
is like the time of Mary at the feet of Jesus;
in the spaces of prayer
love deepens in the heart,
the warmth of God takes hold of the heart,
and we are once again made whole.

This is the time –
time spent with Jesus –
when we can relax into the mystery
of being loved,
of being forgiven,
of being called,
and of being totally held
now and forever,
in love.

SEVENTEENTH SUNDAY IN ORDINARY TIME

Ask and you shall receive.

But I haven't got what I asked for;
I'm still sick, out of a job, without a partner,
marriage hasn't got any better,
all these things we pray for.
And I realise to my pain
that God is no magician.
So much of life I must accept,
so much of life is outside my control.

Will a son speak to me again?
Will a daughter ever again phone home?
Doesn't that depend on them, not just on God?
And still Jesus says,

Ask and you shall receive.

In the asking is the receiving,
in the seeking is the finding,
and in the knocking the door opens,
for in our prayer
God gives the Holy Spirit to those who ask.

We are changed by asking.
What we get in the asking is his gift.
God hears all prayer,
responds to all prayers,
not always the answer we want or expect.
What we receive by asking –
maybe a surge of faith,
an acceptance of love,
a lift of hope,
is what he gives.

In confidence we pray,
and in our prayer
our hand is held,
our anxieties are eased,
our fears are lessened,
and our confidence is that
God always gives the Holy Spirit
to those who ask.

Ask and you shall receive.

EIGHTEENTH SUNDAY IN ORDINARY TIME

To have or to be

The shop window is like a mirror;
we look into it and see something
which we want to possess or buy.
Different things attract different people.
We can almost see ourselves in some of the showpieces –
buy something and we'll appear successful,
buy something else and we may be popular,
something else and we'll look stunning,
something else and we'll be one of the in-group.

Mirrors of possessiveness,
being caught by the attraction of what we might own
and of being looked up to for what we have.

Jesus' story today is about a man who stored it all up,
and then found he had too much to bring with him,
wherever the future might call him.
He was rich in the sight of the world,
and impoverished in the sight of God.

There's a transparency about us all
when we are with God.
All are equally loved in the eyes of God,
just for who each person is,
not for where we live,
or for who our friends are,
or for a youthful body or expert mind.

Loved and valued for who we are,
and how we want to love and care for others,
and how we want to contribute to the world.

All are loved,
and all can make some contribution

to the betterment of the world,
by how we love and give to others.

When we give in love
we lose nothing.
We gain and so
we are richer
in the sight of God.

NINETEENTH SUNDAY IN ORDINARY TIME

Being ready

Being ready and noticing the call of God
is one hallmark of being a Christian.

Be ready
to notice the need of God
in the people we meet:
in their need to be heard at a time of worry,
in their need for care in illness,
for forgiveness when we've hurt each other,
for the conversations
that can bring faith in doubt,
hope in despair
and love always.
For there is the Son of man,
coming at an hour you do not expect.

Be ready, says the Lord,
to notice the need of God
in the millions of hungry children,
homeless parents,
refugees without a home,
people, even children,
sleeping rough in our own cities;
be ready to care,
to help, to reach out,
for there is the Son of man,
coming at an hour you do not expect.

Be ready,
in times and spaces for prayer,
to notice the love of God
reaching you and the world through you,
the forgiveness of God
touching a world of hurt and violence through you,

and the call of God
to be ready
today and every day,
to be his presence, justice and love
among his people.

TWENTIETH SUNDAY IN ORDINARY TIME

Not always a peace-bringer

Jesus talks so much about reconciliation,
forgiveness and love
that we may wonder
about all his words of division.

He says he will not always bring peace,
but because of him people will be divided,
even in families.

Where now is the calm in the storm,
or the offer of rest and refreshment?

We know that we can be divided
about what is right and just.
Families and societies
can be divided about
the cares of life,
the cares of marriage,
the care of the young,
the care of the poor.

In the face of poverty and hunger,
of abuse and violence,
the word of Jesus is divisive,
for it highlights the rights of all,
born and unborn,
rich and poor,
young and old,
sick and well,
to the gifts of the earth,
the gifts of wealth,
and the care of society.

While we love all,

we want justice for all,
and our following of Jesus
may bring division.

May we be encouraged to do what is right,
strong to take the side of God,
and open to reconciliation and compassion for all.

TWENTY-FIRST SUNDAY IN ORDINARY TIME

Through the narrow door

The way to happiness is through the narrow door.
This is the happiness-way of Jesus.

We may think that the way to happiness
is to try everything
and find happiness
through a variety of experiences –
or to possess as much as we can,
and try to find happiness
through wealth,
or to build up acquaintance
with people of the right connections
and find happiness in our circle of contacts –
and Jesus talks
about a narrow door,
and people who are last being first.

He seemed to find happiness
in the way he treated people,
with acceptance and real love,
and with giving his life for them.

That's the sort of happiness he means:
the happiness coming from
commitment to children and family,
and to those in our care,
making the best of failures,
finding spaces and times for prayer
when we know deep-down
joy and peace of soul –
this is the happiness of God,
and this is salvation.

The door to happiness is narrow,

but its foundations are deep;
the door will allow us through
and we can bring in with us
to the dwelling of God
our goodness and generosity,
our prayer and our poverty,

and enter with hands open to receive the gift
of the joy and happiness
of the followers of Jesus.

TWENTY-SECOND SUNDAY IN ORDINARY TIME

Jesus' place at a banquet

When Jesus goes to a banquet –
a wedding reception,
a celebration in the club,
a parish celebration,
he doesn't seem to look for the top table.

He seems to look more in the ordinary places,
to find congenial company
with the person who goes for the lowest place,
with the person who hides behind the pillar,
with the person hanging back to be invited somewhere.

And at the banquet of life
he seems to sit
with those who get the leftovers,
and enjoy their company.

And he is teaching about heaven
as he invites all to the banquet;
we are welcomed by God
for who we are,
for what we have given,
for what love we have created in life,
and tried to give, even with mistakes.

What God praises in us may surprise us:
the simple moments where we have
made a difference in the lives of others,
and big moments where we have made our effort
to help create a world according to the mind of God.

And he embarrassed people
in his own day
by bringing all sorts of people

to the top table.
Maybe he will praise in us
what we least expect.

Sort of turns things
upside down,
doesn't it?

TWENTY-THIRD SUNDAY IN ORDINARY TIME

**Whoever does not carry the cross and follow me
cannot be my disciple.**

Each of us has our own cross to carry;
the weaknesses of body, mind or spirit,
which affect our lives,

or loneliness, illness, failure,
and our personal secret problems.
All of us carry burdens
which are known or unknown to others.

Our cross may be caused by others:
we may be victims of greed and violence,
or of others' addictions.

For the Lord himself carried the cross
of poverty and misunderstanding,
of bereavement when Joseph died,
of loss of friends like Lazarus,
of the pain of his mother as he went to death;
he has carried burdens like ours.

And each cross is different;
at times we feel we could carry another's cross more
    lightly.
And we resent the crosses of our lives caused by others.

The Lord has suffered,
and promises us the companionship we need.
He weeps with us,
suffers with us,
promises friendship
now and forever.

Our way of the cross, like his,

is the path to resurrection.
With our hand in his wounded hand,
we can carry the burdens life brings,
and follow him,
with confidence
and with a helping hand,
to carry the crosses of others.

TWENTY-FOURTH SUNDAY IN ORDINARY TIME

Lost and found

We can lose our way in life;
like when there's failure
and we don't believe in ourselves any more –
in an exam, in a job, promotion,
or feeling a failure as a parent, teacher,
or in whatever is our calling in life.

Loss, bereavement, deep disappointment,
and our faith may be weakened.
We wonder is God really interested,
does he look for us,
search us out like the lost sheep?

Or lost in guilt, remorse, shame
for what stings from the past?

We look for a light in the mist;
like walking home on a foggy night,
wondering will we ever find the way again?

Lost we are at times,
but never without
Jesus Christ,

the one who was lost himself
who suffered bereavement
and all that we suffer.

On the path of our lives,
from first to last moment,
we look on Jesus with thanks –

our guide on the journey
our song in the discord,

our light in the darkness.

Lost in confusion, sin, anxiety,
found in the mercy of the love of God.

TWENTY-FIFTH SUNDAY IN ORDINARY TIME

To what do we entrust our lives?

In each man and woman
is the need and desire for security.
As infants we look to parents totally for security
and as life moves on,
we may look to family, peers, friends and children
for our security,
like rocks on which we feel we will be safe.

And we can entrust ourselves to God,
knowing that words for God
like Rock, Fountain of Living Water, Eternal Life,
are foundations of our security.

Or we may place our trust in
money or financial security,
or prestige and honour from a job,
or entrust our feeling of security to an over-care of the body,
and the question from the gospel of Jesus is:
to what do you entrust yourself?

We cannot place full trust at the same time
in God and wealth,
nor in love and possessions,
nor in a long life and trust in God.

God intends that we use created gifts
like wealth and honour and appearance,
friendship, love and prayer,
to bring us to him;
but if we are entrusted to them,
they may draw us away from him.

May we know the happiness of
entrusting ourselves to God and to love,
and wanting to use all else in his service.

TWENTY-SIXTH SUNDAY IN ORDINARY TIME

Not just a story – Dives and Lazarus

In one of the world's poorest cities
I saw a young boy
selling fruit at the railway platform.
He would make a few pence a day,
enough maybe to stay alive,
and God knows where he would sleep.

The inequality of opportunities in the world,
Dives and Lazarus –
not just a story but real life.

We don't all start life on a level playing field;
some walk uphill from the very beginning,
and Jesus was among the poorest of us.

Our heart must wince
at children who are hungry and homeless from birth,
at people who want a job and cannot get one,
at homelessness, addiction, and any form of abuse;
for parents who cannot give to their children
the best of life and love they wish for them;
for the elderly who are poor and neglected,
and we wonder what can we do.

For we are not the problem:
neither you nor I have caused the poverty of so many,
but we can be part of the solution.

We can join our hearts with the heart of God
and urgently wish to make things better;
we can join our hands to the hands of God
and urgently work to make things better,
and create within parish, neighbourhood, city and world,
places where a more just and caring society is created.

Can we hear the cry of people who feel neglected
so that our hearts are moved with compassion
and our energies moved to give
time, love, and care
to those who need help and support,
for they are the brothers and sisters of Jesus?

TWENTY-SEVENTH SUNDAY IN ORDINARY TIME

Increase our faith

Faith is like a well;
its water is deep, refreshing,
fed by the stream of living water from God;

it started like a trickle of baptismal water,
now it is deeper,
and we draw on it
for meaning, compassion and God's love.

Faith is personal to each of us,
like every child is uniquely loved by parents
in a way that is just for that child.
Faith is like holding God's hand,
and we each hold hands
our own way, with our own unique touch.

Be grateful for faith, the gift of God.
Be patient with its growth.

And let's be confident in its growth.
Through the darkness of doubts,
through the fog of questions,
through the storms of let-down,
faith is nourished, and grows.

Like a stone thrown into the well
immediately upsets the water at the top,
but as it falls it upsets less,
until it hardly disturbs the deep water,
the place of peace and silence,
that place of deep faith,
at the bottom of the well.

For in the bottom of the well is the home of God,

and nobody can destroy that home within us.
In the peace and the silence of its depths
is the living water,
given for ever;
the water that no stone can disturb,
no sin can destroy.

We are grateful for the water that lasts forever,
that springs up inside us for eternal life;
Jesus, the life of God, the life of the world.

TWENTY-EIGHTH SUNDAY IN ORDINARY TIME

Thanks

One day I sat down and relaxed
and went back over the last year:
I thought of all I could be grateful for –
people I met who helped me,
people whom I love and who love me,
the times someone seemed to care.
And I was grateful too
for times I could help another,
show some care,
and make life that bit easier and safer for
family, friends, pupils, colleagues,
and all I contact.

And I thought of health and faith,
for having food on my table,
and enough to live on.

Problems and worries came to mind too:
the worries of others
and my faults and failings,
but in the atmosphere of thanks,
they seemed less intense.

And I know I could go back
over the years and say thanks too,
like a river of thanks flowing by
as I sit and enjoy the memories
and feel the thanks.

Thanks – a word that brings us alive,
for what once was can always give life.
Thanks – a word that keeps us humble,
for we know that we depend on others.
Thanks – a word that keeps us joyful

for we know that in every day
there are the meetings and the memories,
the help and the support,
given and received,
which are the seeds of life and of growth.

May we be people who are truly grateful
to others and to God
for what makes life worthwhile.

Remember this day,
remember last week,
remember all times,
and be grateful!

TWENTY-NINTH SUNDAY IN ORDINARY TIME

Justice for his chosen ones

Anything done in the cause of justice
and in the name of Jesus Christ
will bear fruit in plenty.

Our world suffers much injustice
and our heart pains
when we hear of homeless children,
when we see lines of refugees on our screens,
when we pass someone destitute looking for money,
and our heart pains with something of the pain of Jesus.

We wonder what one person can do?

The call of Jesus spurs us on:
to know that what we do is
one person's effort to
make a more just society,
feed some people who need our help,
educate more widely and care for the sick,
and look after the chosen ones of God.

The path towards justice is
blocked with obstacles of
greed, self-interest, lack of care
and we want to plant that path
with generosity, compassion and care.

For the Lord looks on us
and at the needs of his people
and wants there to be faith on earth.

If our faith is without care for the needy
it is a watered-down faith and is incomplete.

In the strengthening of our desires and work
for the justice of Jesus
our faith in Jesus grows and is strengthened.

THIRTIETH SUNDAY IN ORDINARY TIME

Be merciful to me, a sinner.

Deep down we like to praise ourselves,
and even though we don't say it aloud
don't we sometimes feel we're better than others?

We can list for God
our pilgrimages and fasts,
our holy hours and prayer,
our help to the poor.
and almost want to be praised.

In itself, is that wrong?
Hardly – but it becomes dangerous
when we look down on others.

That's the story today –
the Pharisee was not a bad man,
for he lived a good life
but his fault was
that he looked down on others.

To be at rights with God
is to know that each of us depends on God
for so much in life,
that our faith and religion are gifts,
that our good works and prayer are gifts,
our desire to help the poor is a gift,
and that we should be grateful rather than boastful.

We thank God and others for what we have and are,
rather than for what we do.

In each of us is the humility of the tax gatherer,
and the knowledge that evil finds a home at times in each
    heart –

the evil word and thought,
the evil intention and desire,
the ways we'd like to get even with others;

and there is the willingness to say,
as did the tax gatherer,
'God, be merciful to me, a sinner,'
and know then that
we are at rights with God.
For in the eyes of God
we are, each of us,
sinners who are immensely loved.

THIRTY-FIRST SUNDAY IN ORDINARY TIME

I must stay at your house today.

The Lord wants to stay with us,
close to us,
to become part of our lives.
He comes with a gift,
the gift of salvation,
saying to each what he said to Zacchaeus
'Today salvation has come to this house'.

The gift he brings is
the light of hope to any corners of despair,
the warmth of love to any spaces of hatred,
the confidence that we can face all of life without fear.
His gift is salvation from
fear, despair, hatred,
and his visit heals, strengthens and forgives us.

He does not expect a tidy home,
but a home open to the needs of others;
nor an orderly home,
but a home open to care for others;
nor an up-to-date home
but one open to welcome him.

He comes also with others,
and when Jesus enters our lives,
he invites us to care as he does
for anyone we know in trouble,
and to get involved in the struggle of every
        neighbourhood
for justice, education, health and faith.

Today salvation has come to our lives,
for Jesus has come into our homes,
in the Eucharist and bread of life.

THIRTY-SECOND SUNDAY IN ORDINARY TIME

To him all people are alive.

Coming to the end of life
is like travelling through a narrow tunnel
and when we pass through it at its narrowest,
we then emerge into the widest space we have ever
   known,
wider, brighter
than any of our thoughts, dreams, hopes.

For a true description of God
is the Lover of life,
bringing life to the full,
seeing life when all seems lost,
in despair, hopelessness,
confusion at any age,
or when pain and ill-health drain the body of life.

God looks on our dying moments
and sees not a person nearly dead,
but a man or woman
on the doorstep of full life.

God looks on our times of illness
and sees us struggling with the limits of earthly life
but growing in the life of the soul.

And this is how people saw Jesus:
a man full of the life
of love and of compassion,
of conviction and energy.

One who lived
in the fullness of God's promise
that life is linked
in the golden string

of heaven and earth.

God is not the God of the dead,
but of the living,
and to God,
all people are alive.

THIRTY-THIRD SUNDAY IN ORDINARY TIME

Your endurance will win you your lives.

Isn't courage something we really admire in people?
A child learning to walk and making efforts,
even when she falls or he has to be helped at every step.
A young person trying again after exam failure,
or making yet another job application.
People who make it against the odds
of illness or handicap or deep hurt.
Courage is strength from the inside.

How to nourish this strength?
Look at the face of Jesus
and see the face of God
alive with courage in face of death,
shining with courage in the face of rejection,
a face communicating strength –
strength born in the depths of his suffering –
strength to his friends like you and me when we suffer.

We need courage in love;
when the care we try to offer is rejected,
and we feel let-down and no good;

We need courage when we try to work on behalf
of those who are neglected, homeless, poor,
and our efforts are destroyed by greed in society.

We need courage
in the love which cares for people in pain,
and we feel helpless and angry on their behalf.

Look at the face of Jesus,
alive and shining with courage;
look at the eyes of Jesus,
eyes hopeful with love and friendship,

shining with compassion, for you and me;
an enduring love which is faithful forever.

His endurance won him his life;
he will ensure that our endurance will win us ours.

LAST SUNDAY IN ORDINARY TIME
CHRIST THE KING

And how is he a king?

How is this man a king?
Jesus Christ, of heaven and earth,
mocked and killed through
the cruelty of his people –
a king?

Just in Paradise?
Or now, today?
Where is his power?
How is he powerful?

This man – one single life –
who has been the most predominant influence
on human history.

His power is seen on a cross,
and the cross is his throne.
Maybe we see him at his truest there,
forgetful of self,
mindful of the thief beside him,
compassionate to the end,
saying to the one beside him on Calvary –
'Today you will be with me in paradise'.

His power is in the weakness of love,
and the strength of compassion.
His leadership is in the sharing of struggles
and in his vision of humanity.
His attraction is in his care for all
and in his urgency for justice.
His influence is from the truth of God
and his desire that this word be heard in the way we live.

A king not only of the future but of today,
not only of heaven but of earth,
not of power but of service,
for he comes among us as one who serves.

Compassion, love,
forgiveness, truth,
wholehearted care and acceptance of us all;
this is Jesus the King,
fully human, fully divine,
Son of God and Son of Mary.

FEAST OF THE IMMACULATE CONCEPTION

All is holy.

From the beginning of life,
life is holy and we are holy.

What does it mean –
Mary, conceived without sin?

In this mystery of the beginnings of Mary's life
we glimpse something of the link of
the human and the divine.

In the love of her parents,
in their expression of this love,
she was conceived,
the beginnings of a life
which would welcome God
among his people,
and bring God to birth in a human way.

In the ordinary was the extraordinary,
in the human was the divine,
in human love was divine love:

God's glory in the conception of Mary
and in the love of her parents.

And we are grateful that our human love –
love of marriage, of friendship,
love of the poor and the weak,
love of teacher and pupil,
of God's ministers for his people –
is the door opening to
receive and give the love of God
and to give back to God what God has given,

for when we in love concern ourselves for others,
we are offering to God
what God has given to us –

the love of Father, Son and Spirit,
in the promise of Mary to be
the mother of Jesus Christ,
Son of God, Son of Mary.

THE EPIPHANY OF THE LORD

They brought their gifts.

They brought their gifts:
gold, frankincense and myrrh.

Fit for a king and welcomed by parents.

And what do we bring?

If we think that Jesus later in life
valued the gifts
more than the journey,
then we don't know Jesus.

What he saw was more the way they travelled
than what they carried.
A search for God's way,
following a star,
keeping faith.

Was it not a journey of love?

We bring our love to God.
Love with all its flaws and delights,
its successes and failures.

The love that remained true in difficulties
and the love that once strong grew weak.
The efforts to love are our gift,
as well as the love that worked out well.

The love that died in marriage and divorce,
the love gone wrong in a family,
the love that waned in friendship,
God sees the love of the past
as well as the love of the present.

He looks on our journey of life,
and sees in it the footsteps of love,
the stars that guided us to love
and which guided others through love.
He sees the faithfulness to others
which was a star of the journey.

And the stars of love in our lives
were stars of his making,
for he is the child of love –
the love of Mary, the love of God;
and he is the source of love
for through him all things were made,
through him all love was created
and in him all love is kept in being.

SAINT PATRICK

Traced through time

If you walk a beach you see lines traced in the sands,
remaining there till washed away.
Or the way the sea can change the shape of the coast
with its gentle and rough tides.

Our feast this day
is of one whose lines have not been washed away,
the one who traced the gospel of Jesus
on the shores of a country and shaped its future;

for what he traced in the hearts of people
has remained through centuries
of prosperity and of poverty,
of persecution and peace –

the faith of Patrick and its effects through a history of
    hardship,
the statue of Patrick in younger countries,
where his people shared that faith,
the words of Patrick, a consolation and a spur
to put the concerns of God first in life.

And with Patrick we recall our people
who shared faith and love
in the homes of their own country
and among their own people;
parents, grandparents, extended family,
priests, sisters, brothers,

and men and women who, like Patrick, heard that call
to go among others and share that message
of God's saving love for people;
of education, health and dignity
where those might not be found.

The lines of faith have been traced on many sands,
the gospel has put words on the music of time,
and we are grateful and celebrate
the legacy of one who came in God's name
and of many who lived in God's name.

Patrick's gift was the gospel of Jesus,
our celebration this day
renews our thanks for that gift.

TRINITY SUNDAY

Glory on the face of Christ

The glory of God is on the face of Christ;
the bruised and risen face of Jesus
is God's everlasting glory;
in the death and resurrection of Jesus
is the life of the Spirit sent among us.

And we are his glory,
the glory of God
we carry in earthenware vessels.

As the material of an earthen jar,
or any piece of pottery,
is fragile and can easily be destroyed,
so we carry the glory of God
in our bodies and spirits.

God entrusts
the love and care he has for the world
to the lives of his people.

Each of us
is a space for the Spirit to inhabit,
a place for the Father to live
a face on which the light of Jesus shines.

As a river carries water, we carry God,
as the sun carries light, we shine out God,
as a face mirrors a personality, we mirror God.

This is the glory of God,
Father, Son and Spirit,
the one who is mother and father of us all,
and gives life to all,

one who is saviour and friend
and brings wholeness,
the one who is peace and courage
and brings conviction.

THE BODY AND BLOOD OF CHRIST

In memory of me

Isn't memory powerful?
The mysterious way you can suddenly
remember where you left something,

or the details of a conversation,
or the touch of a hand,
the scent of a rose.
And you remember with feeling;
or you remember the bitter smell of poverty,
the fear of being threatened in any way,
and you recall the event
and relive the feelings.

The feelings and the thoughts –
in the memory.
And the past can become real in the present.

What a life stood for
can be recalled, relived, rejoiced in.

Memory can almost bring a person alive –
people who are absent, deceased.
That's because real life among us is never dead.

'Do this in memory of me.'
In memory of Jesus;
not just a retelling of what he said,
but a reliving of what he did and stood for:

in memory of me and in memory of the living poor,
in memory of me and in memory of the living lonely,
and in memory of the starving and the homeless;

in memory of me and in memory of the ones who came
    for healing,
and in memory of the ones who came for forgiveness;
in memory of me and in memory of the ones who came
    for acceptance
and in memory of the ones who came searching for God.

And in memory of one who died for others.

'Do this in memory of me,'
and remember me alive today
in all who live.
Do this in memory of me.

THE ASSUMPTION OF MARY

The vision of heaven

Mary's summertime feast
expands our vision from earth to heaven,
from time to eternity,
from the human to the divine;

as she is now in heaven,
our sure hope is that one day
we shall share this vision:
to see God face to face,
to live in the circle of love which never ends,
to be alive in the light of joy that never fades.

This is what the human heart longs for,
happiness that will last,
joy that nobody can take from us,
the eternal gift of God.
All that is human is part of heaven,
all that is good, beautiful,
all that is true, all that is alive.

Love that lasts through life,
friendship that does not fade,
the good we do and try to do,
all will live with us in heaven.

Our hope is to bring to God
a life lived in love,
and the effort to live in his gospel,
and to be remembered in kindness and compassion,
and for the good we tried to do
and the love we tried to share.

This feast today
lifts our eyes beyond smoky cities,

to the new and eternal city of God,
attunes our ears beyond any strident cry,
to the silent music of the world's creator,
puts us in touch with the fragrance of God
and the touch of the Father of the world,
gentle, healing, making whole.

This feast today
reminds us all of our immense dignity
as children of God,
a dignity that lasts beyond this life
into the joy and the light of eternity.

We lift our eyes this day
and see the dignity of the one who has gone before us:
Mary, mother of Jesus,
Mary, mother of God.

ALL SAINTS

The vision of God

We look from our village or town
at the sun, the moon or the stars,
and we may be drawn to wonder –
and we are drawn outside ourselves
to something bigger, universal, creative.
For the sun and moon and stars
give light not just to our small place
but to every part of the world.

We need the light of such moments
to draw us into the mystery of
what is universal,
what is mysterious,
what is of God.

Our saints this day
remind us of a life to come.
Our parents, grandparents,
family, friends,
teachers, neighbours, colleagues –
all who have been part of our lives
and who are gone to God –
call us to faith in the life to come,
to hope in the joy of heaven,
and to love that is forever.

Each of those gone to God
is a star to guide us to the light of God,
giving light for the future
and hope for the present.

They are the stars and moon and sun
always shining, always full, always warm,
for they enjoy the vision of God.

And they are still part of our lives,
for we are part of something big and universal,
brightening our lives
with their reflection
of the vision of God,
the joy of heaven,
the light of eternity.